SPORTS

EDITED BY NICK WINNICK

Weigl

CALGARY

www.weigl.com

Published by Weigl Educational Publishers Limited
6325 10 Street SE
Calgary, Alberta, Canada
T2H 2Z9

Website: www.weigl.com

Library and Archives Canada Cataloguing in Publication data available upon request.
Fax (403) 233-7769 for the attention of the Publishing Records department.

ISBN 978-1-55388-494-1 (hard cover)
ISBN 978-1-55388-495-8 (soft cover)

Printed in the United States of America
1 2 3 4 5 6 7 8 9 0 12 11 10 09 08

All of the Internet URLs given in the book were valid at the time of publication. However, due to the dynamic nature of the Internet, some addresses may have changed, or sites may have ceased to exist since publication. While the author and publisher regret any inconvenience this may cause readers, no responsibility for any such changes can be accepted by either the author or the publisher.

Weigl acknowledges Getty Images as its primary image supplier for this title.
Library and Archives of Canada: page 40 top left.

Every reasonable effort has been made to trace ownership and to obtain permission to reprint copyright material. The publishers would be pleased to have any errors or omissions brought to their attention so that they may be corrected in subsequent printings.

We acknowledge the financial support of the Government of Canada through the Book Publishing Industry Development Program (BPIDP) for our publishing activities.

EDITOR: Heather C. Hudak
DESIGN: Terry Paulhus

Sports Inside
Contents

Through The Years

Canada is a nation of sports enthusiasts. Many Canadians grow up playing hockey in the winter, soccer and baseball in the summer, and basketball indoors all year round. It is rare to find a Canadian who does not have his or her own sports story to tell.

When Canadians are not playing sports, they often watch and cheer on professional players. Many Canadians feel a deep bond to their local sports teams, supporting them in tough times and celebrating their triumphs. National Hockey League (NHL) and Canadian Football League (CFL) games draw huge crowds to stadiums around the country.

Canada has a long history of athletic excellence on the world stage. Canadians have won international championships and taken home Olympic gold. Canada's hockey and curling teams have created friendly, longstanding rivalries with other countries around the world, often pushing athletes from many nations to greater heights of performance.

Whatever the future holds, Canadian athletes will continue to thrill and delight people across the country and around the world with their skill. There will be many more unforgettable moments of victory and defeat in the wide world of sports.

Sports
2000s

2002

Scandal in the Judging Booth

In 2002, the world was watching as athletes competed in the Winter Olympics in Salt Lake City, Utah. Figure skating fans were impressed by a pair of Canadian skaters, Jamie Salé and David Pelletier. As the competition wore on, it became clear that the Canadians would be competing against the Russian team of Yelena Berenzhnaya and Anton Sikharulidze for gold. The Russian team skated a difficult routine with only a few flaws. Later, the Salé and Pelletier performed their routine perfectly, receiving a standing ovation from the audience. Even newscasters found it difficult to contain their enthusiasm, saying Salé and Pelletier were likely to win gold. It came as a shock when, despite their perfect routine, the judges narrowly decided to award gold to the Russian team. In interviews, the French judge said that she had agreed, before the competition, to favour the Russian team in exchange for the same favour from the Russian judge in an upcoming competition. She later signed a statement denying this had taken place. The performances were reviewed, and it was decided that the Canadians would receive the gold medal. The Russian team kept their gold medals as well, since it was decided there had been no wrongdoing on their part. This was one of the few times in Olympic history that two gold medals were awarded to teams competing in the same event.

Scandal in the Judging Booth

2001

The majority of the Montreal Canadiens and their arena are bought by American businessman George Gillett.

2002

Canadian men's and women's national hockey teams both win gold at the Salt Lake City Olympics.

Quiet Ice
Gary Bettman

2004

Quiet Ice

The year 2004 will be remembered by many sports fans as the year without hockey. On September 16, 2004, at the beginning of the National Hockey League's (NHL) 88th season, the players went on strike, refusing to play. At the time, players were paid according to contracts they signed with their team. Contracts would promise a set amount of money, no matter how much money that player's team earned. As a result, many teams lost money if they could not sell enough game tickets to cover the cost of player contracts. NHL Commissioner Gary Bettman felt player incomes should be tied to team incomes in order to help teams that were struggling financially. The NHL Players' Association rejected Bettman's recommendation, and a strike was called that kept players off the ice for the entire 2004–2005 season. Eventually, an agreement was reached, and the lockout ended on July 22, 2005, too late to play any of that season's games. This was only the second time in history that hockey's championship trophy, the Stanley Cup, was not presented to a team. When the NHL returned in 2005, its rules had been changed slightly to make the game faster and more exciting for fans to watch. It was hoped that this would allow the league to gain popularity, earn more money, and keep both players and team owners happy.

2003
Edmonton's Chris Benoit wins the WWE's Royal Rumble.

2004
Canucks forward Todd Bertuzzi is suspended.

2005
Steve Nash becomes the first Canadian to win the NBA's MVP award.

7

Even without her long and impressive Olympic career, Wickenheiser would still be in the sports history books. In 2003, her hockey career turned professional. She joined HC Salamat, a men's hockey team in Finland. On January 11 of that year, Wickenheiser became the first woman in history to score a goal in a men's hockey game. Her quest to play professional hockey was not an easy one. Wickenheiser was turned away from an Italian team and declined an offer from an American team before joining HC Salamat. Wickenheiser has also written a book for young readers about her life called *Born to Play*. Her personal motto is "excellence and professionalism."

2008

Fantastic Francophone Fighter

In the early 1990s, a new sport was finding its feet. Ultimate Fighting was a no-holds-barred fighting contest between men. Contestants practised mixed martial arts, meaning that they combined techniques from combat sports around the world, including boxing, judo, karate, kung fu and muay thai. The first Ultimate Fighting Championship was held in 1993, but the league folded soon after. Ultimate fighting critics said that the sport was too violent and brutal to attract advertising. For the next 12 years, ultimate fighting was restricted to small venues,

Hockey Hero

2007

Hockey Hero

Few women are as dedicated to athletics as Hayley Wickenheiser. At just 15, she was selected for the Canadian Women's National Hockey Team. Her great skill as a forward drove her team to capture six gold medals and one

silver at the Women's World Hockey Championships. At the Nagano Winter Olympics in 1998, women's hockey was included as an event for the first time. Wickenheiser and the Canadian team took silver. At the next two Winter Olympics, in 2002 and 2006, the Canadian team took gold medals. Wickenheiser is also a summer athlete, and has a passion for softball. She played for Canada's Olympic softball team at the 2000 games in Sydney, Australia.

2006
Mario Lemieux announces his second retirement from professional hockey.

2007
Canada hosts the FIFA U-20 World Cup.

with little television coverage. However, as time passed, additional rules were put in place, and the sport became less brutal. More fans began attending matches, and in 2005, the league, now called UFC, received dedicated television coverage for the first time. In the late 2000s, Canada made its mark on the sport, thanks to Quebec native, Georges St. Pierre. St. Pierre, a native of Saint-Isidore, wowed audiences and overwhelmed competitors with his exceptional cardiovascular fitness and powerful fighting techniques. St. Pierre went on to win many victories over some of the top fighters, including Matt Hughes, Josh Koscheck, and Matt Serra. In 2008, several sports news outlets ranked St. Pierre as the top welterweight fighter in the world.

Fantastic Francophone Fighter
Georges St. Pierre

Into the Future

Canada has a long history of producing talented fighters in boxing, martial arts, and wrestling. Did you know that modern professional wrestling began in Calgary? What other sports are Canadians known for? Did any others get their start here? What sports do you think will be popular in coming years?

2008

Dylan Barker of Moose Jaw, Saskatchewan, is chosen first overall in the CFL draft, signing with Hamilton.

2009

2010

Sports
1990s

Keeping Gold

Can Canada keep its gold medals? For many Canadians, the announcement that snowboarder Ross Rebagliati had failed his drug test and would lose his gold medal sounded all too familiar. Rebagliati won gold at the 1998 Winter Olympics in Nagano, Japan. It was the first time snowboarding was an official Olympic sport. Although he fought the decision and won back his medal a few days later, Canadians had mixed reactions to the **controversy**. For many,

Rebagliati's argument that he had not used drugs recently was still a national embarrassment. Some remembered their disappointment when rower Silken Laumann failed a drug test and lost her gold medal at the 1995 Pan American games. Canadians sympathized when they found out her failed test was due to a doctor's mistake and a cold medicine that contained a banned drug. Laumann had become a national hero in 1992 when she recovered from a serious rowing accident to win a bronze medal at the Barcelona Olympics. Remembering the international

scandal when sprinter Ben Johnson lost his Olympic gold medal in 1988, Canadians were concerned about the tarnished **reputation** of their athletes.

Dream Teams Enter the Olympics

The 2000 Olympics in Sydney, Australia, saw professional baseball players as part of its competition. By voting to change its amateurs-only rule, the International Baseball Association followed in the footsteps of basketball, hockey, skating, tennis, and cycling. Barcelona's 1992 games were the first to include professional athletes. The American "Dream Team" has dominated basketball at the Olympics ever since. Critics said

Keeping Gold

Dream Teams Enter the Olympics

1991
Ferguson Jenkins becomes the first Canadian inducted to the Baseball Hall of Fame.

1992
The Toronto Blue Jays become the first team outside the United States to win the World Series.

professional participation went against the spirit of the Olympic Games. International competition among hard-working amateur athletes should be the focus, not millionaires gathering to dominate their sport. Many fans seemed to agree. A poll by the American sports network ESPN found that 59 percent of people surveyed said they rooted for the underdog in games against basketball's dream team.

Canada's Game in Trouble

It was about greed, not goals. At least that is how some fans began to see Canada's favourite sport. Hockey turned into big business. In 1990, the average NHL salary was $200,000 U.S. By 1998, the average was well over $1.1 million U.S. It was little wonder that fans had trouble understanding player demands during the 1994 NHL lockout. Canadian teams could not compete with player salaries. Four of the six Canadian NHL teams in the twenty-six-team league sometimes worried more about survival than about strategies for the next game. Since 1996, two NHL teams left Canada for the United States. Quebec City lost its Nordiques to Colorado, and the Jets left Winnipeg for Phoenix. Peter Pocklington, who was at that time the owner of the Edmonton team that was once a hockey dynasty, threatened to sell the Oilers. Some Canadian fans of the sport turned to junior hockey, finding there the excitement the NHL once generated.

Manon Rheaume

Manon Rheaume began tending goal at age seven in Quebec's Atom league. When she cried after getting hurt during a hockey game one day, her father told her, "Macrame isn't painful. Choose!" Rheaume chose and returned to goal. Years later, twenty-year-old Rheaume made hockey history as the first woman to play in an NHL game. Two years after the exhibition game for the Tampa Bay Lightning, she signed a contract with the Las Vegas Thunder, part of the International Hockey League. While few doubted her skill, her small size sometimes held her back from more success in the men's leagues. Critics said that a woman may one day play in the NHL, but it will be a 160-pound woman, not a 120-pound woman. Criticism did not stop Rheaume, who said, "I don't get up every morning to practice just to be the first woman to play hockey. I really like the game."

Canada's Game in Trouble

Manon Rheaume

1993
Ben Johnson is banned from competition.

1994
Hockey is named Canada's winter sport, while lacrosse is re-named Canada's summer sport.

1995
Goalie Patrick Roy leaves the Montreal Canadiens.

11

The Trans-Canada Trail

The Trans-Canada Trail

Not everyone has to be a professional athlete to enjoy sports in Canada. The Trans-Canada Trail was announced in 1994 as a **millennium** project. The 15,000-kilometre trail links every province and territory. Canadians can walk, cycle, horseback ride, cross-country ski, and snowmobile across the country on the network of recreational trails. With the help of a few corporations, the trail was built and funded by volunteers. John Bellini, who was the executive director of the organization that built the trail, said the project was a "perfect fit for the core values of Canadians, the things they have come to care about—clean air, fitness, doing safe and healthy things with their families, and getting back to nature."

1997

Jacques Villeneuve Takes the Prize

"I had to go for it, even if I ended up in the dirt," Villeneuve said, explaining his daring move to reporters. He drove up next to his rival, Michael Schumacher, on the inside lane. Schumacher swerved, hit the back end of Villeneuve's car and crashed off the track. Villeneuve flew past to become the first Canadian to win the 1997 Formula One world driving championship. Sometimes criticized for being too reckless, Villeneuve maintained that, "When you are inside the race car, you believe you control the situation. You have 100 percent confidence in yourself, so you don't think of getting killed." Jacques's father, Gilles, was one of the most famous Formula One drivers in the world. Gilles Villeneuve died in a crash when Jacques was eleven years old.

Jacques Villeneuve Takes the Prize

1996
Wayne Gretzky is traded from the Los Angeles Kings to the St. Louis Blues.

1997
The Toronto Maple Leafs acquire ownership of the Toronto Raptors.

1998
Winnipeg plays host to the Pan American Games.

1997

The World's Fastest Human

It seemed at first like the simplest contest possible. Two men ran 150 metres to see who would win. When the men were sprinters Donovan Bailey and Michael Johnson, however, the contest became a major sporting event watched around the world. The two athletes had developed a public rivalry. Sports fans in more than fifty countries tuned into the race in June 1997. In a few seconds, it was over. Canadian Donovan Bailey won the race and claimed the title as the world's fastest human. Adding the win to his 1996 Olympic gold medals in the 100-metre race and 4 x 100-metre relay,

Into the Future

Many Canadian cities have public recreation facilities, such as parks, hockey rinks, and swimming pools. Some organizations, including the builders of the Trans-Canada Trail, also contribute to health. Are there any places near you that offer recreational activities, such as swimming, skating, or basketball? What other facilities would you like to have nearby?

1999
After 20 years, Wayne Gretzky retires from the NHL.

2000
The B.C. Lions pull out a narrow 28-26 victory over the Montreal Alouettes in the Grey Cup game.

Sports
1980s

The Great One

The Great One

Wayne Gretzky learned how to skate at the age of two on a rink his father made in the backyard. By the time he was six, he was playing hockey with boys five and six years older. During the 1980s, Gretzky was the most exciting player in the National Hockey League. With the Edmonton Oilers, Gretzky won the Stanley Cup four years in a row. He won the Hart Memorial Trophy, given to the most valuable player for the season, for eight years during the decade. In 1989, Gretzky broke Gordie Howe's 1,850-point record of most points scored.

Terry Fox and the Marathon of Hope

On April 12, 1980, Terry Fox dipped his artificial leg into the Atlantic Ocean. It was the beginning of his Marathon of Hope, a run across Canada to raise awareness and funds for cancer. Fox had lost his leg to bone cancer. For 143 days, Fox ran an average of 26 miles a day. He made it two-thirds of the way across Canada before his run was cut short. Fox's cancer had returned—this time to his lungs.

Terry Fox and the Marathon of Hope

Although Fox hoped to beat cancer again and finish his run, he died on June 28, 1981 at the age of twenty-two. Fox had raised $24.2 million for cancer research. More importantly, he inspired many cancer survivors around the world with his spirit. Every year, Terry Fox runs are held across Canada to help raise more money for cancer research.

The Legendary Big Ben

Big Ben is not only a famous bell in London, England. It is also the name of a special horse—the horse was named Big Ben because of its enormous size. In 1983, Canadian show jumper Ian Millar bought Big Ben and brought him to Canada. In 1984, Big Ben came in second place in his first grand prix equestrian competition. Ian and Big Ben were members of the fourth-place team at the Los Angeles Olympics later that year.

The Legendary Big Ben

1981
Abby Hoffman becomes the first woman to be elected to the Canada Olympic Association.

1982
An accident at the Belgian Grand Prix claims the life of Canadian racer Gilles Villeneuve.

During the next decade, Ian and Big Ben won dozens of other competitions. Together, they became the first to win the World Cup title twice in a row, in 1988 and 1989. Big Ben had become a Canadian celebrity. Fans would send him letters and bran muffins—his favourite food. Big Ben retired from professional jumping in 1994. He died in 1999.

1980s

Oil Rush

With Wayne Gretzky as their leader, the Edmonton Oilers were the most exciting team to watch during the 1980s. Gretzky signed on with the young Oilers team when he was eighteen years old. Edmonton was considered a hockey city. The fans were thrilled to get an NHL team. As well as Gretzky, the Oilers team was full of other talented players. Mark Messier, Glenn Anderson, Jari Kurri, and Paul Coffey were some of the league's best players. The young players were full of energy and enthusiasm. They were all good friends who

Oil Rush

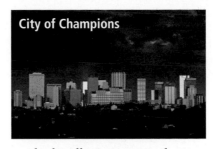
City of Champions

worked well as a team under coach Glen Sather. The team focussed on offensive plays in a league that felt the best teams had strong defensive abilities. The Oilers won the Stanley Cup in 1984, 1985, 1987, and 1988. Hockey fans argue over which team was the best in NHL history. Few disagree that the Oilers of the 1980s were the most exciting.

1980s

City of Champions

Edmonton, Alberta, erected a sign in the 1980s stating it was the "City of Champions" to welcome visitors to the city. In that decade, Edmonton was home to two championship professional sports teams. The Oilers won four Stanley Cups during the decade. In the Canadian Football League, the Edmonton Eskimos also won top honours—the Grey Cup—four times, in 1980, 1981, 1982, and 1987.

1980s

Long-Blooming "Flower"

Guy Lafleur was a right winger for the Montreal Canadiens hockey team from 1971 to 1984.

He was immensely popular with fans because he was such a joy to watch. Stylish, fast, and with drive to win, the "Flower" was one of the most-loved NHL players of all time. Lafleur was a top player from the start of his career. During his rookie season in the NHL, he scored sixty-four points in seventy-three games. He was the youngest player to score 400 goals and also the youngest to reach 1,000 points. Lafleur was also the first player to score more than fifty goals a season in six consecutive seasons. During his career, he won the Art Ross trophy three times for being the league points leader, the Conn Smythe trophy twice for being the most valuable player during the playoffs, and the Hart trophy once for the most valuable player in the regular season. In 1988, Lafleur returned to hockey to play a few games with the New York Rangers and the Quebec Nordiques. He officially retired and was inducted into the NHL Hall of Fame that same year.

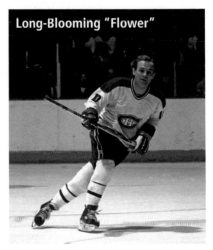
Long-Blooming "Flower"

1983
Torontonian Steve Podborski wins a gold medal at the World Cup of Skiing.

1984
The Edmonton Oilers win their first Stanley Cup.

1985
Steve Fonyo completes Terry Fox's marathon route.

Blue Jay Way

1983

Blue Jay Way

In 1976, Canada got its second professional baseball team. Toronto had wanted a team since Montreal got the Expos in 1968. During their first three years, more than 4 million fans attended the Blue Jays games in Toronto. Despite this support, the team played poorly. Finally, in 1980, the Blue Jays turned their game around. Two years later, under the coaching of Bobby Cox, the team had its best year. In 1983, the Blue Jays had their first winning season, with eighty-nine wins to seventy-three losses. They also set a new attendance record at the Toronto stadium of 2 million fans in a single year. In 1985, the Blue Jays won the American League East championship. The team continued to be one of the best teams in the league throughout the decade.

1985

Man in Motion

Rick Hansen was a world-class wheelchair athlete. Inspired by his friend, Terry Fox, he wanted

Man in Motion

to raise money to help people with disabilities. He decided to travel around the world in his wheelchair. Hansen left Vancouver in 1985 on his Man in Motion tour. He travelled through thirty-four countries, ending his tour back in Canada. His entire trip lasted 792 days. He wore out 117 tires on his wheelchair and eleven pairs of gloves. His Man in Motion tour raised money for research and **rehabilitation** of people with disabilities.

1987

The Olympic Torch Relay

Many Canadians applied for the chance to carry the Olympic Torch as it travelled across Canada to the Calgary Olympic Games. Over 6.5 million forms were sent to the Olympic committee. In the end, 6,520 people were chosen to be torch-bearers. Each torch-bearer travelled 1 kilometre. The torch

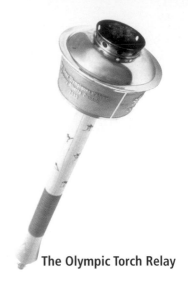
The Olympic Torch Relay

began its journey in Newfoundland in November of 1987. It completed its journey when it reached Calgary to officially open the Olympics. Robyn Perry was the lucky person who was the final torch-bearer. Perry was a 12-year-old student in Calgary. She was chosen to symbolize youth and future Olympians. As two billion people watched on television, Perry carried the Olympic torch up a steep staircase. At the top of the stairs, she reached up and lit the 1988 Olympic cauldron that burned throughout the games. Perry became a Canadian celebrity. For the rest of the year, she made over 100 public appearances talking about her experience with the torch.

1988

Calgary's Olympic Games

In February 1988, the Winter Olympics were held in and

1986
Sport Canada introduces new guidelines for gender equality in sport.

1987
Rick Hansen completes his Man in Motion world tour.

1988
Sudbury, Ontario hosts the World Junior Championship in Athletics.

Calgary's Olympic Games

around Calgary, Alberta. The games brought athletes from around the world. In total, 1,423 athletes from fifty-seven countries participated in the games. The athletes competed in a variety of sports, including ski jumping and ice skating. Calgary and Alberta spent a great deal of money getting ready for the games. A new skating oval was built, as well as Canada Olympic Park, an area with ski jumps and bobsled runs. Thousands of volunteers helped out during the games. The international athletes enjoyed the Canadian landscape and hospitality. The games were a great success.

1988

Drugs in Sport

Canadians watched with anticipation as runner Ben

Drugs in Sport

Johnson became the fastest man in the world. Johnson won a gold medal for the 100-metre race at the 1988 Olympics in Seoul, South Korea. He broke his own world record with a time of 9.79 seconds. It was soon discovered that Johnson had been taking **steroids** to improve his running. Steroids are a banned substance for athletes. Johnson's gold medal and world record were taken away from him. He was banned from competing for two years. His coach, Charlie Francis, had encouraged Johnson and other athletes to take steroids. Francis was banned from coaching for

life. This story made people aware that athletes sometimes took illegal drugs to improve their performance.

2007

The Crazy Canucks

From the mid-seventies to the early eighties, the Canadian National Ski Team was the best in the world. The male members of the team were nicknamed the Crazy Canucks. They included "Jungle" Jim Hunter, Dave Irwin, Dave Murray, Ken Read, and Steve Podborski. The Canadian team dominated downhill skiing like they never had before, or since. A male or female Canadian skier won a World Cup event in every year during the 1980s.

The Crazy Canucks

Into the Future

For many athletes, competing at the Olympics is a lifelong dream. Most Olympians compete for the first time between 16 and 20 years of age. Where will the Olympics be held when you are that age? Do you know anyone who is training to be an Olympic athlete?

1989

The Calgary Flames win the Stanley Cup, defeating Montreal in six games.

1990

The Winnipeg Blue Bombers dominate the Edmonton Eskimos to win the Grey Cup 50–11.

Sports
1970s

Bobby's Run

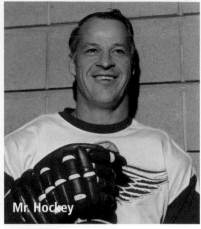

Mr. Hockey

1970s

Mr. Hockey

Gordie Howe played hockey in the NHL for an incredible twenty-six seasons, and he played another six seasons with the World Hockey Association. This brought the total to 32 years as a professional hockey player. In his career with the Detroit Red Wings, Howe was an all-star twenty-one times, was leading scorer six times, and was MVP six times. He retired in 1971, but returned to hockey in 1973 to play in the WHA with his two sons. He fully retired in 1980 at the age of fifty-two.

1970s

A Skater's Skater

Karen Magnussen skated into Canadian figure skating fans' hearts. After winning the women's title at the Canadian Championships in 1968, she had to withdraw from the competition the following year because of leg injuries.

1970s

Bobby's Run

At eighteen years old, Ontarian Bobby Orr joined the Boston Bruins. He was named rookie of the year and proved that he belonged in the NHL. The Bruins had not made the playoffs in three years, but with Orr's help, they won two Stanley Cups and three divisional titles over eight years. Orr won eight straight Norris Trophies as the top defenceman, was MVP three times, and was the first defenceman to lead the league in scoring twice. Knee injuries forced him to retire when he was thirty years old.

1971
The Canadian Rockies Trail Guide is first published.

1972
The Hamilton Tiger-Cats win the Grey Cup.

1973
In an effort to help pay for the 1976 Olympic Games, Montreal announces Canada's first lottery.

A Skater's Skater

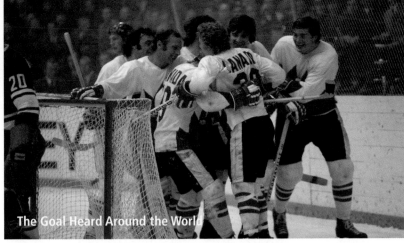
The Goal Heard Around the World

She fought back and regained her title in 1970 and remained the Canadian champion until 1973. Magnussen won silver medals in both the 1972 Sapporo Olympics and the World Championships. She was named the outstanding female athlete from 1971–1973. She was also awarded the Order of Canada.

1970

Ice-cold Competition

Prime Minister Pierre Trudeau kicked off the first Arctic Winter Games in March 1970. The contest involved Inuit games such

Ice-cold Competition
Pierre Trudeau

as hitting cans with a whip, as well as more conventional competitions including basketball and hockey games. The frigid temperatures did not turn anyone away from the fun. The Arctic Winter Games drew about 800 athletes from Alaska, the Yukon, and the Northwest Territories.

1972

The Goal Heard Around the World

The 1972 Summit Series was supposed to be an easy win. No one expected the Russians to give the Canadian hockey team a run for its money, but they did. The Canadians lost the first game, won the second, and tied the third. They were booed off the ice after a 5-3 loss in the fourth game, only to lose the next one, too. The Canadian team had to win all of the remaining games to win the series. They took the next two, so it all came down to the last game. The scoring went back and forth, and the game was tied at 12:56 in the third period.

There would not be an overtime period, and time was running out. With thirty-four seconds left on the clock, Paul Henderson scored with his own rebound. As Foster Hewitt, sports broadcaster, said, it was the "goal heard around the world." It was the most emotional 480 minutes of hockey these professionals had ever experienced. Canadians across the country celebrated the victory, enjoying what would become one of the most remembered, talked-about, and celebrated hockey victories ever.

1974
Racehorse jockey Ron Turcotte is inducted to the Order of Canada.

1975
One of the world's premier equestrian sports facilities, Spruce Meadows, opens in Calgary.

19

The Big "O"

1976

The Big "O"

Montreal's Olympic Stadium, nicknamed the "Big O," was built for the 1976 Olympic Games. It was the first arena to offer both an open and a covered field. A 150-metre tower that stood above the stadium supported an 18,500 square-metre cover that could be lowered over the roof in bad weather. It took until 1987 for the stadium to boast this feature. It cost around $1 billion, making it Canada's most expensive arena of its kind.

1977

Conquering the English Channel

Canadian swimmer Cindy Nicholas was the first woman to swim the English Channel both ways in September 1977. The 20-year-old spent 19 hours and 55 minutes in the water, battling ocean liners' wakes, seaweed, waves, and being battered by shoreline rocks. Her time was 10 hours and five minutes faster than the men's record, and she tied the record for the most crossings by a female, at five. She crossed to the French coast in 8 hours, 58 minutes, two minutes too slow to break the women's record. The next day, two other Canadian swimmers tried to swim the Channel but failed. "The [speed] record wasn't really

Conquering the English Channel

the important thing," she said. "It mattered more to me that no woman had ever done this before. A time is something that can always be beaten. This can't be taken away."

1978

Queen of the Track

Diane Jones Konihowski's dreams came true on August 6, 1978. She won the pentathalon at the 1978 Commonwealth Games in Edmonton, Alberta, with 4,768 points. This set a new record. She won the long jump, shot put, high jump, and hurdles, and came in second in the 800-metre race. Her total has been beaten only once in international competition. The 27-year-old athlete was a landslide victor, with the second place finisher 546 points behind her. Queen Elizabeth II presented Jones Konihowski with the gold medal. She was also named Canada's Female Athlete of the Year in 1978. "I'm too individualistic. On a team you can blame others," Konihowski said of her sport. "I like it better when I win, it's on my own, and if I lose, I've only got myself to blame."

Queen of the Track

1976

Sue Halloway becomes the first Canadian woman to compete in the Winter and Summer Olympic Games in the same year.

1977

The Toronto Blue Jays play their first game, winning over the Chicago White Sox.

1979

High-speed Hero

Gilles Villeneuve's racing style was simple. Whether racing cars or snowmobiles—he gave it 100 percent. Villeneuve won six out of 67 races as a Formula One race car driver, and was considered one of the best drivers ever. Villeneuve began his Formula One career in 1978, driving for Ferrari. He crashed five times in his first six starts, but settled in. He won his first race in 1979 in Montreal and was runner-up as the world's best Grand

Hamilton Home to Hall

Prix driver. His luck ran out in 1982, when he crashed his car and died at the Belgian Grand Prix while driving at 250 km/hour. The Montreal Grand Prix circuit is named in his honour.

October 25, 2007

Hamilton Home to Hall

The Canadian Football Hall of Fame opened in Hamilton, Ontario, in November 1972.

The Football Hall of Fame and Museum was founded in 1962, but was moved to Hamilton, where it remains today. The organization chronicles the history of Canadian football and highlights outstanding players who have played the game. It also recognizes those whose contributions helped build the sport in Canada. The Grey Cup and Schendley Trophy are on permanent display in the Hall.

High-speed Hero

Into the Future

It was common during the 1950s, 1960s, and 1970s for athletes to become unofficial ambassadors of their countries. Athletes are trained to always conduct themselves with respect and sportsmanship. Can you think of ways these traits could be used to help unite countries or people who do not otherwise get along?

1978
Edmonton plays host to the Commonwealth Games.

1979
The World Hockey Association folds, and four teams move to the NHL.

1980
Hockey legend Gordie Howe retires.

1960s

Hockey Cards

Hockey cards have been around since 1910, produced by chewing gum, candy, and cigarette companies. In the late 1960s, trading reached a new high, and some NHL cards sold for hundreds of dollars. The greatest activity still took place in schoolyards across the country, as young collectors scrambled to complete their sets.

Hockey Cards

Ski Queen

1960

Ski Queen

Nancy Greene was Canada's Athlete of the Year in 1968. She began skiing on homemade skis in Rossland, British Columbia when she was three. Her father tied a rope around her waist and helped her along. When she was sixteen, she represented Canada at the 1960 Winter Olympic Games. She finished 22nd in the downhill race. By the next Olympics in 1964, she had climbed to seventh place in the downhill and 15th in the slalom. Her style was fast and aggressive, but she suffered many falls and injuries, including a broken leg. She worked on developing more control of her skiing, and her persistence paid off. In both 1967 and 1968, she won the World Cup. In 1968, at the Winter Olympics in Grenoble, France, she won the gold medal in the giant slalom and the silver medal in the slalom. Her spectacular success brought her many **endorsements** and work as a television sports commentator.

1962

Triple Salchow

At the age of 15 in 1962, figure-skater Petra Burka stunned skating fans by performing the triple salchow during the Canadian Championships. In this jump, the skater spins around three times in mid-air. No other woman had ever before done that during a competition. Petra was coached by her mother, Ellen Burka, who had been a figure-skating champion in

Triple Salchow

1961
The Hockey Hall of Fame moves to a new location in Toronto.

1962
The Grey Cup is played in fog so thick that the last 10 minutes had to be completed the next day.

Holland. Encouraged by her success, Petra trained hard and won several international awards. In 1964, she won the Canadian Championships and a bronze medal in the Olympic Games. Her best year was 1965, when she won the Canadian, North American, and World Championships, and was awarded the Lou Marsh Trophy as Canada's outstanding athlete. In 1966, she gave up competitive skating and turned professional, skating in ice shows.

1964

Northern Dancer Wins Kentucky Derby

On May 2, 1964, Northern Dancer was the first Canadian racehorse to win the Kentucky Derby, the most famous horse race in the world. The course is 2 kilometres long, and Northern Dancer ran it in 2 minutes flat. No horse had ever run it faster. That same year, he won the Preakness Stakes, another big race in the United States, and the Queen's Plate in Toronto. Crowds cheered him. Many people said he was one of the greatest Canadians ever. After he hurt his leg, his owner, E.P. Taylor of Windfields Farm, built him a comfortable place to live, and he fathered around 150 colts. Some of his children were great racers, too, but none was as fast as Northern Dancer.

1965

Beliveau at the Helm

Jean Beliveau was the most successful captain of the best hockey team, the Montreal Canadiens, during the 1960s. He learned to skate in his backyard in Victoriaville,

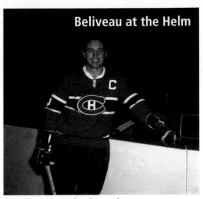
Beliveau at the Helm

Quebec, and played junior hockey in Quebec City. In 1953, he moved to the Canadiens. Over the next seventeen seasons, he scored 79 goals in playoff games. As captain for 10 years, he also won the Stanley Cup a record five times. He earned the respect of both his teammates and the club management. "I always tried to solve things right in the dressing room," he said, "without getting management involved." He carried extra money to help players out on tour, listened to their problems, and smoothed out arguments. In 1965, he was the first winner of the Conn Smythe Trophy for most valuable player. Beliveau's large size lent him to be a dominant figure on the ice. Players who tried to check him said it was like bumping into an oak tree—they just bounced off. He quickly summed up a situation in the game and used his excellent stickhandling to take advantage of it. Fans called him "Le Gros Bill" after a French-Canadian folk hero.

Northern Dancer Wins Kentucky Derby

1963
Sam Jacks of North Bay, Ontario, invents ringette.

1964
Betsy Clifford becomes the youngest Canadian skier ever to compete in the Olympics.

1965
Steve Yzerman is born in Cranbrook, British Columbia.

Swimmer Wins Big at Commonwealth Games

1966

Swimmer Wins Big at Commonwealth Games

Elaine Tanner set a record at the 1966 Commonwealth Games in Kingston, Jamaica. She won four gold and three silver medals. Her specialties were the backstroke, butterfly, and individual medley. She also swam freestyle on the relay team. Elaine was only 15 years old and barely 5 feet tall, but her triumphs earned her the nickname "Mighty Mouse." On the final day of the games, a group of Canadian fans chanted M-I-G-H-T-Y M-O-U-S-E as she sped through the water. She was named Canada's Athlete of the Year—the youngest ever to get that award. Her career was spectacular but short. At the Pan-American Games in Winnipeg in 1967, she won two gold and three silver medals,

Professional Golf

smashing three world records. The next year, at the Olympic Games in Mexico, she won two silver medals and a bronze. At the age of 18, she quit competitive swimming. In 1971, she was inducted into Canada's Sports Hall of Fame.

1966

Professional Golf

Sandra Post was Canada's first female professional golfer. Between the ages of sixteen and eighteen, she won the Canadian Junior Girl's Championship. She was determined to excel in her sport. In 1966, she moved from Ontario to Florida so she could practise year-round. Two years later, she entered the Ladies' Professional Golf Association Championship. Amazingly, she won the tour in her rookie year. Her success led many other Canadian amateur golfers to turn professional.

1966
Bobby Hull sets the record for the most goals scored in a single NHL season.

1967
The Toronto Maple Leafs defeat the Montreal Canadiens, winning their last Stanley Cup to date.

24

1967

Hockey Night in Canada

In 1967, Dolores Claman, a young jingle composer, was asked to write a rousing theme for *Hockey Night in Canada*. She came up with two melodies, and the one selected opened the show for many years. It has even been called Canada's unofficial national anthem. Centennial Year was a good one for Claman. She also co-wrote A Place to Stand, the Ontario theme song for Expo 67. The *Hockey Night in Canada* theme was used by the CBC for 40 years, until 2008.

Academic Athlete

Hockey Night in Canada

1969

Academic Athlete

Russ Jackson has been called the finest professional football player of all time. In high school, he excelled in both academics and sports, winning all-star honours in basketball, baseball, and football. While at McMaster University, he won the Governor General's Medal for Excellence. He joined the Ottawa Rough Riders in 1958 and quickly became the team's best quarterback. A strong runner and an excellent passer,

he played for eleven years. In that time, he completed 1,341 passes, and 184 for touchdowns. He also scored 55 touchdowns himself. In 1969, he led his team to the Grey Cup championship. He won the Schenley Award as outstanding player three times, and the Lou Marsh Trophy as Canada's athlete of the year. At the same time, he taught high school, and after he retired from football, he became a school principal.

Into the Future

Hockey plays an important part in the Canadian sporting identity. People play hockey, and variations, such as ball hockey, field hockey, and ringette, all across the country. Can you think of any other sports that are played in various ways? How could you put a twist on your favourite sport to make it just a bit different?

1968
Montreal sports journalist Elmer Ferguson is inducted to Canada's Sports Hall of Fame.

1969
The Montreal Expos play their first home game.

1970
The Vancouver Canucks join the NHL.

Sports
1950s

Canadian Pairs at the Top

1950s

Canadian Pairs at the Top

Canadian pairs figure skaters were the best in the world in the late 1950s and early 1960s. Both Barbara Wagner and Robert Paul were late starters in figure skating. Wagner began at 13 and Paul at 10 as part of his recovery from childhood polio. Wagner and Paul dominated the scene, remaining world champions from 1957 to 1960, and winning the gold medal at the 1960 Olympic Games. Not far behind Wagner and Paul were the brother and sister pair, Maria and Otto Jelinek. The Jelineks had immigrated to Canada from Czechoslovakia with their family after World War II. The Jelineks won the Canadian junior pairs title in 1955, and in 1962, they won the world championships. Both pairs had the reputation of being dedicated professionals.

1950s

Marlene Stewart

"No other Canadian golfer, man or woman, has ever run up a series of victories comparable to hers," wrote sports columnist Jack Batten. Marlene Stewart started working as a **caddy** when she was 12. She loved the sport as soon as she tried it. The club's pro once commented that he could not go into the pro shop without tripping over Marlene's shoes. She got her first hole in one when she was 15. The rest is

---

1951
The first colour television sports broadcasts are made.

1952
Canada's men's hockey team wins gold at the Olympic Games in Oslo, Norway.

1953
Hockey player Lanny McDonald is born in Hanna, Alberta.

Marlene Stewart

gold history. Between 1951 and 1973, Stewart won the Canadian Ladies' Open Amateur championship eleven times. In 1956, she won 34 matches in a row. These wins included the Canadian Open and the United States's Amateur championship. A journalist once said: "She is a perfectionist...she has hit more golf shots, mostly in practice, in her three years in the game than the vast majority of women golfers have hit in the last 10."

1950

Canada's Best All-Round Athletes

Lionel Conacher, the "Big Train," was chosen Canada's all-round athlete of the half century in 1950. Canada's all-round female athlete of the half century was Bobbie (Fanny) Rosenfeld.

Canada's Best All-Round Athletes

The Big Train was an obvious choice. He had made his name in wrestling, boxing, football, lacrosse, baseball, and hockey. Sometimes, he played in two different games on the same day, dashing from one to the other. One story says that he helped the Toronto Hillcrest team win the Ontario baseball championships by hitting a triple in the final inning. He then drove across town to help his lacrosse team with the championships. He scored four of his team's goals. Conacher later played professional football and hockey. Bobbie Rosenfeld also shone at numerous sports, including softball, basketball, hockey, track and field, and tennis. She won the 1924 Toronto grass-courts tennis title and set new records for the broad jump. Her peak performance was in the 1928 Olympic Games, when she won a silver medal in the 100-metre dash and a gold medal in the 400-metre relay. One admirer recalls: "She was not big, perhaps five-foot-five. She didn't look powerful but she was wiry and quick. Above all she was aggressive, very

Grey Cup on the Small Screen

aggressive physically....She simply went after everything with full force." In later life, she wrote a sports column called "Sports Reel" for the *Globe and Mail*.

1952

Grey Cup on the Small Screen

On November 29, 1952, the Grey Cup game was shown on television for the first time. More than 700,000 fans were able to watch the Toronto Argonauts play the Edmonton Eskimos at Varsity Stadium in Toronto. The picture was clear, but it failed during the third quarter. Fortunately, the sound was not affected. The announcer continued to describe the game while a technician climbed a 100-metre tower to repair a receiver. The picture came back 29 minutes later, in time for viewers to see the exciting finish. The score was Argos 21, Eskimos 11.

1954

The Miracle Mile, a showdown between distance runners Roger Bannister and John Landy, took place in Vancouver.

1955

The Canadian Sports Hall of Fame is created.

1954

Marilyn Bell Swims Lake Ontario

"I'll never say a woman can't do anything in future," said a Toronto taxi driver. Sixteen-year-old Marilyn Bell had just done what no one else had ever managed. She had swum across Lake Ontario, a distance of 52 kilometres. Americans and Canadians had been trying to cross the lake for years. Nobody dreamed that a Canadian high school student would be the first to succeed. Entering the water at midnight on September 8, 1954, Marilyn swam through the rest of the night and all the next day. She struggled ashore near the Canadian National Exhibition grounds on the evening of September 9. Marilyn was so exhausted that she was hardly aware of the cheering crowds who had gathered to greet her. The radio had been broadcasting news of her progress, and 250,000 people had flocked to the waterfront to celebrate her arrival.

1955

Riot Ends Hockey Game

On March 17, 1955, angry hockey fans went wild at the Montreal Forum, hurling eggs, tomatoes, and peanuts at Clarence Campbell, the National Hockey League president. Campbell had suspended Maurice (Rocket) Richard

Riot Ends Hockey Game
Clarence Campbell

for attacking a player and a linesman the previous Sunday. The fans were outraged at this treatment of their idol. They became so violent that the game had to be stopped. As they poured out of the Forum, they were joined by thousands of other angry Montrealers. The mob spread along St. Catherine Street, smashing shop windows and anything else in their path. By midnight, more than 100 people had been arrested.

1956

Rowers Take Gold

A four-oar crew from British Columbia won a gold medal at the Olympic Games in Australia in 1956. This was the first time Canada had ever won an Olympic rowing event. The four members of the crew were Don Arnold, Lorne Loomer, Walter d'Hondt, and Archie McKinnon. Until a few months before the event, only 21-year-old Don

1956

Lucille Wheeler wins an Olympic bronze medal. She is the first Canadian to win an Olympic ski medal.

1957

Rick Hansen is born in Port Alberni, British Columbia.

Rowers Take Gold

mask he had been using at practice games. No goalie had ever worn a mask at a regular hockey game, and Blake was against it. Nevertheless, Plante won the argument—and the Canadiens won the game. From then on, Plante always wore a protective mask when he was in goal. Soon, other goalies began to do so, too.

Arnold had any rowing experience. The other three were 19 and had never rowed before. They were trained by former rower Frank Read, an outstanding coach. "He is fantastic the way he can inspire us," said Walter d'Hondt. "He makes us want to do anything for him." The crew members rowed from 5:00 to 6:30 a.m., worked all day as construction workers, and then rowed another hour and a half in the evenings. On weekends, they rowed long distances under the watchful eye of Read. Of the remarkable success of his team, Read commented that "it was the most phenomenal effort ever made in international competition."

1959

A First for Goalies

With blood pouring from his face, goalie Jacques Plante was helped off the ice. The puck had hit him square on the nose. "We've had it now," muttered a Montreal Canadiens fan. There seemed to be nothing left to stop the New York Rangers from sweeping to victory. The Canadiens had no spare goalie for that game on November 2, 1959. As Plante sat in the dressing room while the cut on his nose was sewn up, coach Toe Blake tried to persuade him to go back on the ice. Plante refused. He said he would only go back if he could wear the

A First for Goalies

Into the Future

Today, NHL goalies always wear a mask, but in the 1950s, many did not. Jacques Plante took a stand and helped make others aware of the importance of wearing a mask. Can you think of any ways to improve the rules, game play, or equipment used in your favourite sport? How can you share these ideas with others?

1958	1959	1960
The frisbee is invented.	The first World Curling Championship is held.	Gordie Howe takes Maurice Richard's place as the leading scorer in NHL history.

Edmonton Grads Move On

Edmonton Grads Move On

The Commercial Graduates Basketball Club began as a women's high school team. The Grads, as they became known, dominated women's basketball from 1915 until 1940. They rarely lost a game and won 49 out of 51 titles. They won the Underwood International Championships 23 times—they had not lost it once. Among the list of the Grads' accomplishments was the French and European Championships as well as the North American Championships. By the time the team retired, there were only 48 players listed for the 25-year life of the team. The team attracted gifted athletes who stayed with the club for as long as they could. The women were more than great basketball players. They were also representatives of Edmonton. They were hailed as a Canadian institution and promoted Canada abroad. Dr. James Naismith, the inventor of basketball, called them "the finest basketball team that ever stepped out on a floor."

1940

Marathon Runner

Gèrard Côté trained in Quebec, running more than 50 kilometres in a session. He competed in the famous Boston Marathon, which drew runners from all over North America. In 1940, Côté won the race by nearly four minutes. In 1943, he received permission for leave from the Canadian army to run the marathon again. He and an

Marathon Runner

American soldier ran the race together, each wearing army T-shirts. Côté beat his friend by less than two seconds. The following year, there were only 69 men in the race—most healthy men were fighting the war. People did not think that Côté should be allowed to race while others were dying in Europe. The army barred any soldier from participating in non-military athletics. Côté took personal leave from the army. He ran the race and won his third Boston Marathon. The army was not impressed. As soon as he finished, Gèrard Côté was shipped overseas. After the war, he won the marathon yet again in 1948.

1940

Joe DiMaggio, American Hero

"Jolting" Joe DiMaggio was the greatest outfielder ever to play the game. People thought he was good enough to replace Babe Ruth when he entered spring training in 1936. He did not disappoint. He played professional baseball for 13 seasons. His style of play was smooth and easy, both in the field and at the plate. He had great statistics, and he hit 28 home runs a year, despite battling injuries. DiMaggio owned the Yankee's outfield, and no one ever doubted that. In 1941, Joe DiMaggio had a 56-game hitting streak, and finished

1941
Joe DiMaggio is named Associated Press Male Athlete of the Year.

1942
The Toronto Maple Leafs win the Stanley Cup.

1943
Canadian high jumper Diane Gerace is born.

Joe Dimaggio, American Hero

Maple Leaf Legend

the season with 30 home runs and 125 runs batted in. He also had pride in his country. He took a three-year break in 1943 in order to fight in the war. Joe DiMaggio tested the imagination of American baseball fans as well as those who never watched the game. DiMaggio was nearly a mystery. He did not speak openly with the press, so details about his personal life were not easy to come by. He married silver-screen goddess Marilyn Monroe in 1954. She was a woman about whom every man dreamed and who every woman envied. They divorced later that year. Songs and books in the 1960s and 1970s spoke of the impact Joe DiMaggio had on the United States. He remains an American sports legend even after his death in 1999.

1942

Maple Leaf Legend

Syl Apps was an Olympic pole vaulter before he joined the Toronto Maple Leafs hockey team in 1936. He was team leader in scoring and was the Rookie of the Year. He won the Lady Byng trophy for sportsmanship in 1942, and was either a first- or second-team all-star centre five times. He had seven successful seasons with the team, acting as team captain for most of his career. In 1943, Apps took a break from his hockey career to join the Canadian army. He picked up where he left off when he returned from overseas, and led the Leafs for another three years. He retired in 1948. At the end of his career, Apps had 201 goals, 432 points in 423 games. In recognition of his achievements, Syl Apps was inducted into the Hockey Hall of Fame in 1961.

1943

Hockey Hall of Fame Honours Achievement

Canada's unofficial national sport was finally officially honoured in 1943. The Hockey Hall of Fame was established to honour the excellent athletes and administrators in the game. The players, officials, and builders of hockey who made great contributions to the game were remembered in the Hall. Hockey artifacts displayed at the Hall included goalie masks, sticks, trophies, and international hockey sweaters. A selection committee of media and people who know a lot about the game chose the players elected to the Hall. The Hall of Fame also served to promote the sport in the Canadian community. The Hockey Hall of Fame was first built at the Canadian National Exhibition (CNE) in Toronto. It was founded by the National Hockey League, the Canadian Amateur Hockey Association, and the City of Toronto. While the CNE buildings were being built, the Hall shared space with Canada's Sports Hall of Fame. It has since moved to a location in downtown Toronto.

Hockey Hall of Fame
Honours Achievement

1944
Joe Nuxhall, age 15, becomes the youngest player to pitch a Major League game.

1945
Maurice Richard sets the NHL record for goals set in a single season.

31

1943

Longden Wins the Triple Crown

John Longden's career lasted 40 years and was crammed with achievements. He won more than 6,000 horse races. Only 10 other jockeys in history have enjoyed that many victories. Longden and his family lived near Taber, Alberta, where he worked in the coal mines during the week and raced horses on the weekend. He visited Salt Lake City, Utah, in 1927, and won a race on a horse named Hugo K. Asher. That began his successful career as a jockey. Longden trained and rode a horse called Count Fleet. In the 1930s and early 1940s, Longden won three Louisiana Derby races. In 1943, he won the Kentucky Derby, Preakness, and Belmont Stakes with Count Fleet. His greatest achievement also came that year. He rode the horse to victory at the prestigious North

American **Triple Crown**. These accomplishments earned him a spot in the National Museum of Racing's Hall of Fame in New York. After retiring, John Longden trained horses. His most famous horse was Majestic Prince, which went on to win the Kentucky Derby.

1944-1945

Number Nine Hits Number Fifty

Maurice "The Rocket" Richard was one of the Montreal Canadiens' most loved players. After battling injuries, he scored 32 goals in his first full season. In the 1944–45 season, Richard scored 50 goals in 50 games—a record that was enthusiastically celebrated. In the last game of the season, "The Rocket" scored on the Boston Bruins, and even the Bruins fans cheered and gave him a standing ovation. The players closest to Richard in the scoring race had only 29 goals for the season. He led the league in goals five times. Despite his incredible goal-scoring ability, "the Rocket" never had the assists needed to clinch the league scoring title. He won the Hart Trophy for the Most Valuable Player in 1947. Many times, he scored several goals in a game. Richard scored three goals in a game for a hat trick, and he scored four goals in a game twice. He scored all five goals in a 5–1 victory over Toronto in 1944. Many of his records remained unbroken until the 1980s.

Number Nine Hits Number Fifty

1946

Breaking Colour Barriers

Jackie Robinson was the first black man to play major league baseball. He joined the Montreal Royals farm team in 1946. He played out his career with the Brooklyn Dodgers. The team challenged the unwritten rule banning black baseball players from playing in the major leagues, but Robinson knew that

Longden Wins the Triple Crown

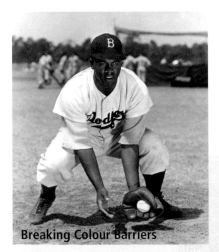
Breaking Colour Barriers

1946
Vincent "Manny" McIntyre of Fredericton, New Brunswick, is the first African Canadian to sign a professional baseball contract.

1947
Barbara Ann Scott wins the World Figure Skating Championships.

he would not be welcomed by the Dodgers' players or fans. In 1947, Robinson played his first major league game. More than 26,500 fans came to watch. He hit his first home run in April. When he returned to the dugout, none of his teammates shook his hand. Despite this, he continued to play well. By the season's end, Robinson was ranked second to Bing Crosby as the "Most Admired Man." Two years later, Robinson and three others became the first black players to play in the all-star game. Robinson opened the door for other black baseball players to make it to the major leagues.

1947

Canada's Golden Girl

Canadians watched in awe as Barbara Ann Scott skated to the top. The 18-year-old girl from Ottawa won the World Figure Skating Championship on February 16, 1947. It was the first time a Canadian had earned the honour. She beat out 21 other skaters from seven countries to win the title, but Scott was not finished yet. The next year, in St. Moritz,

Canada's Golden Girl

Switzerland, she became the first Canadian to win a gold medal in figure skating at the Olympic Games. She overcame ice that was rough after a hockey game, and she performed flawlessly. She out-skated 24 other women from around the world. After Barbara Ann Scott finished her routine, the fans cheered and had picked their favourite to be the gold-medal winner even before the rest of the skaters had competed.

1948

Grey Cup Fever

In 1948, the Calgary Stampeders broke the East's hold on the Grey Cup. They met the Ottawa

Rough Riders in the big game and won, but this was not an ordinary year. For the first time, the Grey Cup final was not just a football game. It now involved a festival that lasted for a week before the contest. It had become a national celebration. Calgary fans' enthusiasm spread. The Stampeders' logo was a horse, and the fan club brought a dozen horses to Toronto. They rode a horse through the Royal York Hotel in downtown Toronto. Aboriginal chiefs attended in full traditional costume. There were chuckwagons shipped out by train. The Stampeders' supporters served pancake breakfasts from the back of them. Calgary fans brought the West to the East and came home victorious. The Grey Cup was the most watched sporting event in the country.

Grey Cup Fever

Into the Future

In 1948, one of Canada's largest sporting event, the Grey Cup, turned into one of Canada's largest parties. The tradition of Grey Cup parties continues today, with many cities across the country hosting festivities. Host cities are named ahead of time, to give people time to prepare, travel, and make arrangements. Where will the Grey Cup be held this year?

1948
The Toronto Maple Leafs win the Stanley Cup.

1949
Canada defeats Denmark at the World Hockey Championships.

1950
The World Hockey Championship is won by the Edmonton Mercurys.

1930s

Boxers Not Boxed In

Boxing was popular in Canada. It ranked third in sports coverage behind only hockey and baseball. Some of Canada's boxers were also great performers. Jimmy McLarnin, for example, was a welterweight fighter who would do a forward somersault after knocking out his opponent. McLarnin was voted Canada's best boxer of the first half century. Boxing offered young men an escape from slums. A preliminary bout paid $50, and even amateur boxers earned $5 a fight. Heavyweight champions earned more money than most famous baseball players and the best-paid football coaches. Boxers were often poor boys who had been fighting for honour and survival on the street for most of their lives. Ethnic fighters created pride in their communities. Jewish boxers showed their toughness, contradicting stereotypes that Hitler and the Nazis spread through propaganda. Barney Ross, a Jewish boxer, said he felt as though he was fighting for all Jews. Many Jewish boxers wore the Star of David on their trunks. Promoters played on the ethnicity of the boxers—Ross was "the Hebrew Challenger," and when Max Baer fought Max Schmeling, the fight was called "Jew versus German."

1930s

Ada Mackenzie

Ada Mackenzie was Canada's best female golfer. She won the Canadian Ladies' Amateur Open in 1919, 1925, 1926, 1933 and 1935. Later, she captured the Canadian Women's Senior Golf Championship eight times. Mackenzie was an innovator in women's golf clothing and established Ada Mackenzie Ltd., a successful women's clothing store in Toronto. While playing in the U.S. Women's Amateur Championship, she decided that her clothing was not suitable for golfing. "I was wearing wool,

Boxers Not Boxed In

Ada Mackenzie

1931
Maple Leaf Gardens opens its doors to Toronto hockey fans.

1932
The Toronto Maple Leafs win the Stanley Cup.

1933
The first recorded fatal skiing accident in the Canadian Rocky Mountains occurs.

The Business of Golf

my sleeves were down over my wrists and the skirt was sloughing in the mud. It was just the completely wrong outfit. I lost the match but it was that experience that got me into the ladies' sportswear business."

1930s

The End of Montreal's Hockey Rivalry

The Montreal Maroons catered to the English Canadians in Montreal and enjoyed a natural rivalry with the French-favoured Montreal Canadiens. However, when the two Montreal teams traded players, the illusion of bitter rivalry became hard to maintain, and attendance at the games fell. The Maroons pleaded for assistance, but the NHL refused to help. The Maroons collapsed in 1938, just three years after winning the Stanley Cup.

The End of Montreal's Hockey Rivalry

1930s

The Business of Golf

The cost of golf clothing, green fees, equipment, and caddies limited the number of people who played golf during the Depression. Most people thought golf was a gentleman's game. The game was popular among businessmen, who closed business deals as they played and later socialized in the clubhouse. Although golf was fashionable in every province, it was more popular in large, urban areas. The Alberta Golf Association promoted golf in rural areas by arranging tours of top golfers. It also allowed members of small town golf clubs to play at urban clubs. Ontario and Quebec dominated Canada's golfing scene. More women golfed in the 1930s than previous decades. There were no professional tournaments for women. Golfer Marjorie Kirkham of Montreal was an exception to the rule. She captured the 1930 Canadian amateur title, and the following year, she reached the finals of both the Canadian open, which anyone could compete in, and the closed, in which a player needed an invitation. In 1932,

she won the Canadian Ladies' Open championships. She then became the first female teaching pro in North America.

1930s

Lady Bessborough Trophy

Many women played hockey in the 1930s. Although the Canadian Intercollegiate Women's Ice Hockey League collapsed in 1933, women's teams from every region of Canada challenged for the Lady Bessborough Trophy that was donated in 1935 for the national championship. Female leagues included teams of factory workers, department store clerks, telephone company operators, and secretaries. Outstanding teams included the Red Deer Amazons, the Edmonton Rustlers, the Montreal Maroons, and the Summerside (Prince Edward Island) Crystal Sisters. The Preston Rivulettes won 348 of 350 games during the decade and captured the Lady Bessborough Trophy six times.

Lady Bessborough Trophy

1934	1935
Canada takes part in the British Empire Games in London, England.	The Winnipeg Blue Bombers win the Grey Cup, becoming the first western CFL team to do so.

Blood on the Ice

1934

Blood on the Ice

In 1934, Toronto Maple Leaf "Ace" Bailey's hockey career, and almost his life, was ended when an Eddie Shore body check cracked his skull. The incident took place at the Boston Gardens on December 12, 1933. Late in the game, "King" Clancy checked Eddie Shore against the boards in the Boston end. Shore thought that Bailey had checked him. Skating down the ice at full speed, Shore spotted Bailey resting on his hockey stick. Approaching Bailey from behind, Shore hit him in the kidneys with his right shoulder. Bailey somersaulted backwards and hit his head on the ice. Seeing his teammate injured, Red Horner skated up to Shore and punched him in the jaw. According to one witness, Shore's head hit the ice,

"splitting open. In an instant, he was circled by a pool of blood about three feet in diameter." By now the crowd was in an uproar. Police had to restrain the fans as the Leafs retired to their dressing room. Newspapers carried daily bulletins as Bailey had two operations for his fractured skull. Toronto fans called Shore an animal, and demanded that he be banned from hockey for life. Bailey's father bought a gun and took the train to Boston, where he intended to even the score. Bailey recovered, but his career was over.

1935

Winnipeg Takes the Cup

In 1935, with only four Canadian-born players, Winnipeg captured the Grey Cup by defeating Hamilton 18-12. Western Canada had won its first Grey Cup game. "You should have been in Winnipeg that afternoon," a local magazine wrote. "Radios set out in the snowy streets blared of Winnipeg's triumph to shouting, cheering crowds. Moviegoers bellowed thunderously as the news was announced in theatres." The team was the

Winnipeg Takes the Cup

"toast of the town." However, the league was unhappy with the way Winnipeg had created such a powerful team. In February 1936, it ruled that no team could employ more than five non-Canadian players.

1937

Hockey Heroes

The public eagerly followed the careers and personal lives of such sports personalities as Lionel Conacher, Syl Apps, Frank Boucher, Joe Primeau, Francis "King" Clancy, and Ivan Johnson. Aurel Joliat, the idol of French Canada, usually wore a black baseball cap when he played. "King" Clancy, a 147-pound, hard-hitting hockey defenceman with a fiery temper, could whip crowds into a frenzy.

Hockey Heroes

1936

Earl Bascom of Alberta creates the first rodeo arena for the U.S. state of Mississippi.

1937

Bradford Washburn and Robert Bates become the first to climb Mount Lucania, the third-highest mountain in Canada.

Howie Morenz was nicknamed "the human projectile" for his habit of throwing up his arms and spinning into a spreadeagle collapse on the ice in an attempt to draw a penalty on an opposing player. His reckless style and headlong rushes up the ice earned him a reputation as the Babe Ruth of hockey. When Morenz died in 1937 from a blood clot as a result of crashing into the boards, 200,000 people lined the parade route to the cemetery in Quebec.

1938

Eddie Shore

The best hockey showman was Eddie Shore of the Boston Bruins. Shore's rushes up the ice brought fans to their feet. Shore accumulated almost 1,000 stitches, fourteen broken noses, and five broken jaws during his career. In Boston, he was a hero, while on the road he was a villain who often led the league in penalty minutes. Thanks to an adoring press, everyone knew that Shore liked to travel alone and only drank water in containers sent from Canada. In 1938, when the Bruins rejected his contract demands, Shore refused to play. Finally, with the fans chanting "We want Shore! We want Shore!" the team had to bring him back. The start of a Boston game was pure entertainment. After both teams had warmed up, the lights were lowered, and the crowd grew silent. Two ushers appeared at the entrance to the rink. One carried a talcum-powdered hockey stick; the other held the gate open for Shore. As Shore stepped on the ice, a spotlight illuminated him, the loudspeakers blasted out "Hail to the Chief," and the crowd broke into a deafening roar. Sporting a black and gold cape, and accompanied by a valet, Shore blew kisses to the fans as he slowly circled the rink.

Eddie Shore

Into the Future

Hockey and boxing gained great popularity in the 1930s thanks to the colourful personalities of the athletes who competed in these sports. Think about athletes today. Do any stand apart from others for reasons other than their athletic skills? What makes this person special? How is he or she a role model?

1938
Canadian track and field athlete Siegmar Ohlemann is born.

1939
The Northern League championship is won by the Winnipeg Maroons.

1940
The racehorse Seabiscuit wins its final race.

Sports
1920s

Women's Rules

Golden Age of Sport

Canada was sports-mad in the 1920s, and the media helped make the 1920s the golden age of sports. Newspapers promoted all sporting events. They counted on sports pages to attract readers. Eighty percent of men said they read at least a part of the sports section each day. Popular journals ran articles by well-known sports writers Ted Reeve and Lou Marsh. Radio and films helped create a mass appeal for sports. Cinemas showed films of famous boxing matches and provided highlights of important sporting events before feature films. **Wire services** such as CP and UPI made it possible for Canadians across the country to be equally well informed of regional, national, and international events. Media coverage of sports was as central to the game as were the athletes themselves. In most cases, famous coaches and athletes owed their status to the journalists who wrote about them.

Golden Age of Sport

Women's Rules

Because women were considered physically inferior to men, their games were made easier in the 1920s. In women's softball, the distance between bases was shortened, and women could not slide into bases. Track-and-field meets did not include the discus or the pole vault, and women ran shorter distances. Volleyball and badminton required fewer points for women to win, and female golfers teed off closer to the hole. In general, female rules limited physical contact and restricted the players' movements. The rules of basketball also reflected these beliefs. Although many women wished to play by male rules, most parts of the country believed that such rules tended to develop aggressive characteristics rather than proper female behaviour. Women's basketball rules, called Spalding Rules, discouraged all physical contact. The court was divided into three areas. To reduce running, only three players per team were allowed in each area, and players could not change areas. No more than two dribbles could be made before the ball had to be passed to a teammate.

1921
"Behave Yourself" wins the Kentucky Derby.

1922
The Toronto St. Pats win their first Stanley Cup.

1923
Pete Parker calls the world's first play-by-play radio broadcast of a hockey game.

league's most valuable player. Sports writers compared Morenz to the American baseball hero Babe Ruth. Morenz had speed, power, and style. It was said that he could stop on a dime and leave a nickel in change.

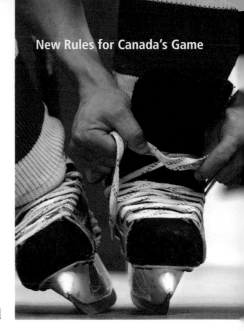

Lords of the Rink

1920s

Lords of the Rink

The 1920s was an era of hockey heroes—Eddie Shore, Aurèle Joliat, Georges Vézina, Frank Boucher, the Cook brothers, and Howie Morenz. Morenz was the best player of his day. He helped the Canadiens win the Stanley Cup in 1924, twice led the league in scoring, and won the Hart Trophy three times as the

1920s

Athletes and Entertainers

During World War I, African-American baseball teams crossed the border to play Canadian teams. Such "barnstorming" teams as the Cuban Giants played more than 300 games in the Maritimes, and their players became household names. To attract fans, African-American teams exaggerated Canadians' misconceptions about them. The players deliberately spoke with southern accents, threw the ball behind their backs, sat in chairs on the field, or threw to the wrong base before throwing to first to get the runner out. Canadians of African descent also played baseball, although they were usually forced to play on all-black teams and leagues. Slowly,

black players were admitted to community baseball leagues.

1922

New Rules for Canada's Game

Hockey was different in the twenties. Until 1922, minor penalties took players from the ice for three minutes. The most important difference was the offside rule. A forward pass to a teammate that crossed the blue line was offside, and the play was stopped for a face-off. Players had to stickhandle across the blue line. Until 1928, it was also illegal to pass the puck forward inside the opponent's blue line. This made for frequent stoppages of play and low-scoring games. In the 1928-29 season, for example, Montreal Canadiens goaltender George Hainsworth had 22 shutouts in 44 games.

Athletes and Entertainers

1924

Earl Bascorn of Alberta creates the first one-handed bareback horseriding rig.

1925

The Victoria Cougars are the last non-NHL team to win the Stanley Cup.

Lionel Conacher

1922

Lionel Conacher

Lionel Conacher was Canada's best and most popular male athlete. He helped the Chicago Blackhawks win the Stanley Cup, was a star halfback in the Canadian Football League, and led the professional lacrosse league in goals. He also played baseball in the International League, wrestled professionally, was the Canadian light-heavyweight boxing champion, and shot an amazing game of golf. In the 1922 Grey Cup game, Conacher scored 15 points on 2 touchdowns, a drop-kick field goal, and two single points. He then left the game after the third quarter to play in a hockey game. Lionel Conacher went on to write a regular sports column for a Toronto newspaper under the by-line "Canada's Greatest Athlete."

1924

Beginning of the Grads

The Edmonton Grads was Canada's most successful womens' team. From 1915 to 1940, it won 502 of 522

basketball games in Canada, the United States, and Europe. Coached by Percy Page, some players were well-known across Canada. In the 1924, 1928, 1932, and 1936 Olympics, the team won every one of its games. Playing in long stockings, bulky blouses, and with ribbons around their foreheads to keep their hair in place, the Edmonton Grads won seventeen consecutive North American championships.

1925

The NHL Expands

At the start of the decade, three leagues competed for the Stanley Cup—the Pacific Coast Hockey Association, the Western Canada Hockey League, and the National Hockey League. Almost every team was based in Canada. When the NHL began to expand into the United States, the teams in smaller towns could no longer compete. In 1925, the Boston Bruins became the first American team in the NHL. The Bruins dressed in brown and gold, which was the colour of owner Charles Adams' grocery chain. Although Boston won only six of its thirty games, the team

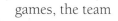
Beginning of the Grads

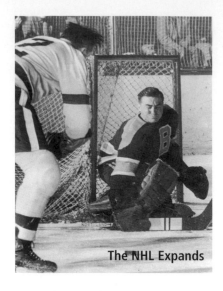
The NHL Expands

was a financial success. The next year, William Dwyer bought the Hamilton Tigers, moved it to the new Madison Square Garden, and renamed the team the New York Americans. A year later, four more American teams were members of the NHL. To sell tickets, American sports writers emphasized hockey's violence. One famous columnist claimed that hockey was played by "men with clubs in their hands and knives lashed to their feet." By 1927, only the NHL teams were left to compete for the Stanley Cup. The league now consisted of ten clubs: two each in New York and Montreal, and one each in Ottawa, Toronto, Detroit, Pittsburgh, Boston, and Chicago. The next year, the New York Rangers became the first American NHL team to win the championship.

1926
Canadian long-distance runner Paul Collins is born.

1927
Babe Ruth sets a Major League record, hitting 60 home runs.

1926

Diamond Days

Baseball was the most popular sport in Canada. Its popularity reflected the growing influence of American culture in Canada. Crowds gathered in front of newspaper offices to watch the World Series games illustrated on a scale-model diamond. An announcer over a loud speaker recreated the action provided by wire services. Every community had an amateur baseball team. Toronto won the Little League World Series in 1926. The Montreal Royals and the Toronto Maple Leafs played in the International League, which was one step below the majors. One study of Canadian sports pages in the decade revealed that approximately half of the coverage of baseball discussed American baseball teams. America's heroes became Canada's heroes, too. Baseball bats sold in Canada were marketed under such names as Ty Cobb and Babe Ruth.

1928

Fanny "Bobbie" Rosenfeld

Fanny "Bobbie" Rosenfeld excelled at every sport she tried. She played on championship basketball teams, won the Toronto tennis championship, threw the discus and the javelin, ran the hurdles, and shone in hockey and softball. The 1928 Olympics were the highlight of Rosenfeld's career. She was a member of the Canadian relay team that won the gold medal, and she won the silver medal in the 100-metre race, just missing first place. However, it was her fifth-place finish in the 800-metre race that showed the

Fanny "Bobbie" Rosenfeld

kind of person she was. She had not trained for this race, but the track coach entered her so that she could encourage her 17-year-old teammate, Jean Thompson. In the stretch run, Rosenfeld ran beside Thompson and when the teenager began to falter, she urged her on. Nearing the finish line, Rosenfeld let her teammate finish fourth.

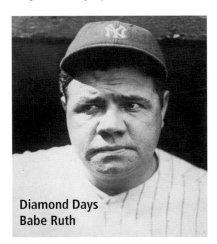

Diamond Days
Babe Ruth

Into the Future

Basketball gained popularity in many cities because it can be played almost any place and does not require much equipment. Being able to play indoors certainly helps during Canadian winters. Are there any other sports that are easy to play indoors or outside? How did these sports begin? Where are they played today?

1928

The first six Canadian women allowed to compete in the Summer Olympics win four medals.

1929

The Boston Bruins win the Stanley Cup.

1930

The Montreal Canadiens win the Stanley Cup.

Sports
1910s

Olympic History

League Leader

1910s

Olympic History

During the 1910s, the flag with five interlocking rings that has come to symbolize the Olympics was created. It would not be flown until the 1920s because World War I interrupted international athletics. The 1912 Olympic Games were the first to host athletes from all six continents. Athletes from around the world went to Stockholm in 1912 to compete in the fifth summer Olympics. There were 2,541 participants in total, with fifty-seven of them being women. Canada sent only half the number of athletes it had to the previous Games in London, and it won half as many medals. Regardless, Canadian athletes claimed three gold medals, two silver medals, and three bronze medals.

1910s

League Leader

Hockey in the 1910s brings to mind many names, especially Maurice (Joe) Malone. Malone played for the Montreal Canadiens. He was the league's lead scorer on several occasions. Malone scored nine goals in a Stanley Cup game in 1913. He scored eight in a Stanley Cup game against the Montreal Wanderers in 1917, and seven in another championship game against Toronto in 1920. In the 1918 season, Malone scored 44 goals in only 20 games. He went down in the NHL history books with records that remain unbroken.

1910s

Sporty Women

Women who wanted to take part in athletics faced some unique obstacles. To swim, they wore bathing dresses that came to their knees, with bloomers attached to them. Tennis outfits were down to their ankles, but women were sometimes allowed to leave their hats off for purposes of the sport. In 1919, Suzanne Lenglen caused a stir when she competed at the Wimbledon tennis championship

1911

The world's first national park service, Dominion Parks Branch, later called Parks Canada, is created.

1912

The first Calgary Stampede, a rodeo and agricultural exhibition, is held.

Sporty Women

hatless wearing a light, white, calf-length skirt that exposed part of her leg as she played.

1911

Golden Swimmer

George Hodgson was a university student at McGill University in

Golden Swimmer

Montreal. He was also the best swimmer in the world, and Canada's first Olympic swimming champion. In 1911, as a warm-up for the Olympics, Hodgson competed at the Festival of the Empire Games in England. He set a new world record for the one-mile (1.6 kilometres) race. During the heats of the 1,500-metre freestyle at the 1912 Olympic Games, the 18-year-old broke another world record only to break it again. Before he was finished, he had broken the record again in the final race and won the gold medal. Hodgson had beaten his closest opponent by 39 seconds. Along the way, George Hodgson also broke Olympic records for the 1,000-metre race and the mile race. A few days later, Hodgson won another gold medal in the 400-metre freestyle race, breaking yet another world record in the semi-final race. His records stayed intact until 1926. After Hodgson competed without success in the 1920 Olympic Games, he retired from the sport.

1917

Birth of the NHL

In 1917, the National Hockey League was born. There were four teams in the new league—the Montreal Canadiens, the Montreal Wanderers, the Toronto Arenas, and the Ottawa Senators. The first season did not work out as well as planned. The Montreal Arena burned down, so the Wanderers had to disband because they did not have anywhere to play. In the end, the Montreal Canadiens and the Toronto Arenas played for the title. Toronto won the first game 7 to 3, and Montreal took the next game 4 to 3. The two-game playoff was based on total goals, so the Toronto team was named the "Champions of the World." It was a challenge to fill arenas and rosters during the war, but the NHL managed to survive its rocky start. It soon added more teams, including American teams from Detroit, Boston, Chicago, and New York.

Birth of the NHL

1914
Canada enters World War I, cancelling many sporting events.

1916
Earl Bascom competes in a steer-riding event that launches him into international fame.

1917
The NHL is founded in Montreal.

43

Sports
1900s

1900s

Flame-Fighting Star

The 1900s was the decade of the marathon—long races were the craze. Robert Kerr had speed, which was enhanced by his involvement in the fire department. Kerr was trained as a firefighter in Hamilton, Ontario. He used his speed to win three races ranging from 100- to 950-metre stretches at the Coronation Games in 1902. He could not afford to compete at the 1906 Olympics in Athens, but he was able to run at the 1908 Games in London, England. Kerr won the 240-metre race and came in third in the 110-metre competition. His medals and his record in the 60-metre race made him a natural

choice for the 1912 Olympics, but Kerr decided instead to retire. He remained involved in track and field by managing the Olympic team.

1900s

Brutality of Boxing

In 1900, fighting was illegal in North America. Boxers avoided the law by fighting in remote areas. Boxing exhibitions, or sparring demonstrations of the "manly art of self-defence" were legal. In 1910, Canadian boxer Tom Foley fought the last four rounds of a fight with his left arm hanging at his side because he had broken a bone in his wrist. The last bare-knuckle fight in North America was in Halifax in 1901. To earn money, boxers fought as often as

possible. Sam Langford of Nova Scotia fought nearly 600 times. He once had three bouts in three different rings on the same night. Tommy Burns was Canada's only heavyweight champion. Born Noah Brusso in Vancouver, Burns weighed only 73 kilograms. After winning the title in 1906, Burns defended it ten times, defeating the national champions of England, Australia, and Ireland. In 1908, he agreed to fight Jack Johnson in Australia. This would be the first time that an African American had been allowed to fight for the heavyweight championship. On Christmas Day, Johnson knocked Burns out in the fourteenth round.

1900s

Baseball Boom

Baseball was Canada's most popular sport. One prairie pioneer remembered: "Everything in them days you could say was baseball ... when you was gonna have a game you'd chase the town crows off the pasture and scrape up the

Baseball Boom

Flame-Fighting Star

Brutality of Boxing

1901	1903	1905
The Winnipeg Victorias win their second Stanley Cup.	The world's first rodeo arena and grandstand are built in Raymond, Alberta.	The Ottawa Senators win their third Stanley Cup.

cow plops and that was about it." During the decade, an average of eight Canadians played on major league teams in the United States. Winnipeg supported a professional team that played in an American mid-west league. Toronto, Montreal, and Vancouver all fielded teams in international leagues.

1900

Development of Football

The modern game of football was still evolving. It was called rugby-football. In 1900, teams played with 14 players, the centre used his heel to kick the ball back to the "quarterback," and there was no forward passing. There was also no blocking past the line of scrimmage, and a touchdown, termed a "try," was worth four points. In 1905, the value of a touchdown was increased to five points, teams were reduced to twelve players, and to retain possession of the ball, teams had to make 10 yards in three downs. Football made another change in 1909. The first ever Grey Cup game, named after Governor General Earl Grey, was played. It became a symbol of

Canadian football. The University of Toronto defeated the Toronto Parkdale Canoe Club 26 to 6 before 3,807 fans to win the Cup. Western teams did not compete in the Grey Cup until 1921 when the Toronto Argonauts beat the Edmonton Eskimos 23 to 0.

1904

The Original Old-Timers

The best hockey team of the decade was the Ottawa Silver Seven, which won the Stanley Cup in 1903, 1904, 1905, and 1909. The most unusual Stanley Cup took place in 1905. During this year's playoffs, eight members of the Yukon Nuggets travelled 7,500 kilometres from Dawson City to Ottawa to play against the Silver Seven. They had planned to take dog sleds to Whitehorse, but there was a lack of snow. The hockey players had to walk and bicycle the 60 kilometres carrying all their gear. When they arrived in Whitehorse, a blizzard trapped them in the hotel for three days. To complete their journey, the players then had to board several ships and trains. The trip took 23 days. The tired

Nuggets lost the series by scores of 23-2 and 9-2. One newspaper wrote that the team faded away like a snowball beneath a June day's sun.

1906

The Unbeatable Tom Longboat

Thomas Longboat was born on the Six Nations Indian Reserve in Ontario. As a long distance runner, he was unbeatable. He won the Hamilton "Around-the-Bay" race in 1906, the Toronto Ward's Marathon from 1906-1908, the Boston Marathon in 1907, and the World's Professional Marathon Championship in 1909. After competing in the 1908 Olympics, Longboat became very popular as a performer in the professional racing circuit. After he turned pro, he improved his 15-mile record time by 7 minutes. During World War I, Longboat continued to race while also serving as a dispatch runner in France. He lived most of his life in Toronto, but returned to the Six Nations Reserve in 1944, where he died five years later.

Development of Football

The Original Old-Timers

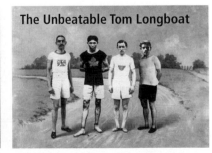

The Unbeatable Tom Longboat

| 1906 | 1910 |

1906
Tommy Burns becomes the first Canadian to win boxing's Heavyweight Championship.

1910
The first Grey Cup match is won by the University of Toronto.

45

ACTIVITY
Into the future

S ince humans have been on Earth, they have played sports and games. Sports are invented by creative people who are looking for ways humans can interact with their environment in fun and challenging ways. There are many different types of sports, but most have some basis features in common.

An important part of any sport is a set of rules for play. Some sports, such as running or skateboarding, only need rules when athletes come together to compete with one another. Most team sports, however, must be played within a specific set of rules. Baseball, soccer, and basketball are examples of team sports that have firm rules in place. Rules may include penalties for people who behave poorly during the game or standards by which points are scored.

Another important part of any sport is its equipment. Some sports require very little gear. For example, track athletes need only have a good pair of running shoes. To play full-contact sports, such as football or hockey, athletes must wear full sets of pads and protectors. Balls of all shapes and sizes are common, as are specialized play items such as pucks and badminton shuttles.

Spread Your Message

Think about the sports you play on a team or as an individual. What are your favourite parts of each sport? What equipment do you need to play? Are there special rules for the game? Now, try putting these pieces together to form a new sport. Many great sports have been created by making small changes to existing sports. Your sport could involve a change to the rules of a game you know already. What if you could use your hands in a soccer match or replace a football with a frisbee or hula hoop? Making these changes to sports you know well can create an entirely different pastime. You also could try inventing a new sport. To do this, imagine how your sport will be played and the equipment you will need. Is it a team sport, or do people play as individuals? How many people or teams take part in each game? Will you need special equipment, such as protective gear or a ball? Once you have made a set of rules, try testing your invention by playing with your friends.

FURTHER
Research

Many books and websites provide information on sports. To learn more about this topic, borrow books from the library, or surf the Internet.

Books

Most libraries have computers that connect to a database for researching information. If you input a key word, you will be provided with a list of books in the library that contain information on that topic. Non-fiction books are arranged numerically, using their call number. Fiction books are organized alphabetically by the author's last name.

Websites

To learn more about sports in Canada, visit **www.tsn.ca**.

For interactive sports information, surf to **www.sikids.com**.

Glossary

caddy: a person who carries a golfer's clubs

controversy: at the centre of a dispute

endorsements: products a person supports for profit

millennium: a period of 1,000 years; often used in reference to the year 2000

rehabilitation: work done to restore a person to good health

reputation: the beliefs or opinions that are held about something or someone

steroids: drugs that help athletes improve their performance; most competitions do not allow athletes to use these drugs

Triple Crown: when a baseball player leads in home runs, runs batted in, and batting average in a season

wire services: organizations that collect news stories and distribute them to newspapers and other media

Index